11+ English Creative Writing

WORKBOOK 4

Stephen C. Curran

Edited by Andrea Richardson and Warren Vokes

Sub-editor: Katrina MacKay

This book belongs to

Accelerated Education Publications Ltd.

Contents

7. Grammatical Devices   **Pages**

1. Nouns — 3-14
2. Pronouns — 14-15
3. Adjectives — 16-17
4. Conjunctions — 17-18
5. Verbs — 19-20
6. Adverbs — 20-22
7. Prepositions — 22-23
8. Interjections — 24

1st Draft of Story 7 'The Spooky Mansion'
1st Draft of Story 8 'The Old Tombstone' — 25-34

8. The Seven Structure Steps

A. The Beginning — 35-36
    1. Set Up — 36-38
    2. Emotional Hook — 38-40
    3. Provoking Incident — 40-42
Beginning of Story Summary — 43-49

B. The Middle — 50
    4. Tipping Point — 50-52
    5. Crushing Reversal — 52-54
Middle of Story Summary — 55-60

C. The End — 61
    6. Big Climax — 61-67
    7. After Effects — 68-69
End of Story Summary — 70-74

Summary of Story Structure Steps — 75-76

2nd Draft of Story 7 'The Spooky Mansion'
2nd Draft of Story 8 'The Old Tombstone' — 77-86

Chapter Seven
Grammatical Devices
Parts of Speech

Words are the writer's toolbox. Words can be classified into eight **Parts of Speech**. Words are named according to their function or use in a sentence. This means a word can appear in more than one category, depending on how it is used.

**Nouns • Pronouns • Adjectives
Conjunctions • Verbs • Adverbs
Prepositions • Interjections**

1. Nouns

A **Noun** is a naming word. Nouns are used to name:

People • Animals • Places • Things • Abstract ideas

a. Common Nouns and Proper Nouns

Common Nouns
These refer to the name of **a person** (boy, aunt, mother, girl), **a place** (school, building, country, house), **a thing** (pencil, ink, eraser, satchel) in a general sense.

They are not written with capital letters.

Proper Nouns
These refer to the name of **a person** (Trevor Smith), **a place** (Rome), **a thing** (Oxford Dictionary), **days of the week** (Tuesday), **months of the year** (March), **titles of people** (Lord Argyle), **organisations** (The United Nations) in a specific sense.

They are always written with a capital letter.

Example: Identify the use of Common Nouns and Proper Nouns in *'The Christmas Lights'* story.

'There was a loud cheer, then all the **elves** clapped and danced for joy. Everyone fell silent and the crowd parted. Two elegantly dressed elves in purple tunics processed towards the **podium**. They carefully removed the golden **crown** from its central position and placed it on a crimson **cushion**. Then they approached **Angie** in a regal and solemn manner.

Santa drew alongside Angie, "This is the moment we've all been waiting for and what better way to celebrate **Christmas**."

"What's happening? Look, I'm just an ordinary **girl**. I'm not special."

"Wrong my dear. You're going to be the **queen** of **Lapland**. An ancient legend says that, one day, a **Princess Angelina** would come to rule the kingdom of the elves, and here you are!"

Angie started to speak, "But I..."

"Don't be embarrassed, it's your birthright."'

Exercise 7: 1

In the above passage of *'The Christmas Lights'* there are six Common Nouns and six Proper Nouns highlighted. Sort these Nouns into the correct categories below.

Common Nouns

1. .... 2. .... 3. ....

4. .... 5. .... 6. ....

Proper Nouns

1. .... 2. .... 3. ....

4. .... 5. .... 6. ....

b. Collective Nouns and Possessive Nouns

Collective Nouns

These refer to the name given to a **group of persons** (choir of children, staff of teachers, cast of actors, class of pupils), **things** (fleet of ships, collection of paintings, bundle of sticks, clump of bushes) or **animals** (gaggle of geese, litter of kittens, shoal of fish, hive of bees).

These Nouns can be single words e.g. jury or committee.

Possessive Nouns

In the **Possessive** case a Noun changes its form by use of apostrophe and s (**'s**) to show that it owns something else.

Rule: Always try to add 's to the possessor of the object.

Example 1: The possessor of the bag is the girl.
In the sentence **The bag belonging to the girl.**
we can add **'s** to **girl** so we can now shorten the sentence.
It now becomes **The girl's bag.**

Example 2: The possessors of the bags are the girls.
In the sentence **The bags belonging to the girls.**
we can add only the **'** (apostrophe) to **girls**. We drop the **s** otherwise it will turn **girls'** into **girls's**, which will sound odd.
It now becomes **The girls' bag.**

Note: A common mistake is to simply add **'s** (apostrophe s) for singular and the **'** (apostrophe) for plural Possessives. In the following two examples **'s** (apostrophe s) is added in both the singular and the plural form.

Example 3: The possessor of the clothes is the man.
In the sentence **The clothes belonging to the man.**
we can add **'s** to **man** so we can now shorten the sentence.
It now becomes **The man's clothes.**

Example 4: The possessors of the clothes are the men.
In the sentence   **The clothes belonging to the men.**
we can add **'s** to **men** so we can now shorten the sentence.
It now becomes   **The men's clothes.**

Note: Sometimes the possessor of the object is written at the end of the sentence, but it still takes **'s** (apostrophe s).

Example 5: The possessor of the luggage is the teacher.
In the sentence   **The luggage of the teacher was lost.**
we can add **'s** even when the sentence is written like this.
It now becomes   **The lost luggage was the teacher's.**

Example: Use a variety of Collective Nouns and Possessive Nouns in *'The Christmas Lights'* story.

'Before Angie could say another word, the music struck up. A band of clockwork soldiers, playing flutes, trumpets, drums and tambourines, marched out from a doorway. **The faces of the elves** *beamed with glee as they paraded up and down the hall, keeping in perfect step. A herd of reindeer followed, led by Prancer,* **the favourite of Santa**. *A group of bad-tempered looking trolls kept the reindeer in line.*

Santa yelped with delight, "The anthem for the Queen of Lapland. At last, the Kingdom of Lapland is secure."

The soldiers stopped playing. Swarms of fairies flew through the windows and hovered over the elves. Tiny elf children played tag and darted in and out of every gap and through **the legs of their parents**. **The hats of the children** *kept falling off because they dodged about so quickly. The smallest elf child naughtily ran right into* **the walking stick of an elderly elf** *and the old elf tumbled into* the crowd of unsuspecting trolls. They fell over like a pack of cards.

Timmy apprehended the naughty elf child and started to scold it, but **the tears of the child** soon made him soften and stop. He gave the child a quick cuddle and released it. By now the whole company of elves was cheering and everyone was jostling to get just a glimpse of Angie. The only face not smiling was Angie's.

Santa lifted his hands. Everybody fell silent. Then the elves gazed in awe as Santa lifted the crown from the cushion. The elves gasped in wonder at **the magnificence of the crown**. As Santa held it high above her head, Angie looked up. The cluster of jewels in the golden crown glistened, but the huge diamond in the middle was the most dazzling. It was surrounded by sapphires, rubies and emeralds which shot rays of coloured light in every direction.

The face of Santa with his warm, inviting eyes again came into focus. Through the blinding haze of reflected light, Angie could see his lips moving, but she couldn't make out his words. Angie sensed her legs begin to wobble and she felt very dizzy. She strained even harder to hear, and then the hall began to spin. Round and round it went until everything became a blur.'

Exercise 7: 2

In the above passage of *'The Christmas Lights'* there are eight Collective Nouns. Write these Nouns in the spaces below.

1. .... 2. ....
3. .... 4. ....
5. .... 6. ....
7. .... 8. ....

Possessive Nouns in their longer form have been highlighted in *'The Christmas Lights'* story. These longer forms need to be converted into the shortened version.

e.g. *'the favourite of Santa'* becomes *'Santa's favourite.'*

Write the shortened forms of the other Possessive Nouns.

1. .... becomes ....
2. .... becomes ....
3. .... becomes ....
4. .... becomes ....
5. .... becomes ....
6. .... becomes ....
7. .... becomes ....

c. Concrete Nouns and Abstract Nouns

Concrete Nouns

These refer to names you give to anything or anyone that can be perceived through the physical senses of **Sight** (house, pen, paper, ship), **Hearing** (bells, alarm, whistle, explosion), **Touch** (rough, smooth, cold, hot), **Taste** (sweet, sour, bitter, spicy), **Smell** (stink, perfume, aroma, musty).

Note: Concrete Nouns can be perceived by more than one sense at a time. e.g. soap can be seen, touched and smelt; a sandwich can be seen, touched, tasted and smelt.

Abstract Nouns

These refer to the names of **Ideas** (freedom, justice, hope, power, time), **Feelings** (love, hate, jealousy, admiration, relaxation), or **Qualities** (curiosity, trust, deceit, bravery, tenacity). None of these things can be perceived through the physical senses, but they still exist. They are the opposite of Concrete Nouns which can be perceived through the senses.

> **Example:** Use a variety of Concrete Nouns and Abstract Nouns in *'The Christmas Lights'* story.

'Suddenly a deafening voice boomed in her ears, "Make a wish and it will come true."
Angie felt queasy and light-headed. She knew she was going to pass out. She had this feeling before when she went to her new school. The children left her on her own when they went to lunch. Not a single person spoke to her from the moment she arrived right through to when she went home. She felt really alone and nobody wanted to be her friend.

The voice came again, gentler this time, "Make a wish and it will come true."
Angie summoned all her strength and wished with all her might for the one thing that mattered to her above all things. She wished she had just one friend; that's all she wanted. For a moment everything came into focus. The heavy crown now rested on her head and she felt the weight of it. Everybody was cheering, then Santa patted Angie on the shoulder and nodded with approval.

Santa bent down, "Would Queen Angelina like to address her new subjects?"
Angie looked around the sea of faces, but, as usual, there was no one there she could really call her friend. In this new place she had admirers, but they were not friends. There was only Timmy; he stood on his own, apart from the others. He obviously had no friends either. She tried to catch his eye but he seemed lost in his thoughts. Then the aching loneliness returned and gnawed away at her insides. It was closely followed by the feeling of nausea returning. Angie slumped forward and everything went black.'

© 2008 Stephen Curran

Exercise 7: 3

From the passage of *'The Christmas Lights'* story, write down six Concrete Nouns and six Abstract Nouns.

Concrete Nouns:

1. .... 2. .... 3. ....

4. .... 5. .... 6. ....

Abstract Nouns:

1. .... 2. .... 3. ....

4. .... 5. .... 6. ....

d. Using Nouns Creatively

Using a fuller range of Nouns in your stories helps stimulate various kinds of description. **Noun Strings** can be used as descriptive aiming points in a passage to ensure every kind of Noun has been utilised and to help you generate ideas.

Example: Create a Noun String that forms the basis for extending the *'Aliens'* story and then write it.

The Story So Far

'Kim fell back terrified as the bright lights grew closer. The forest lit up and the hum became a deafening wail. She crouched down behind the bushes and shielded her eyes. Suddenly the blinding light faded and there was silence. A large, disc-like shape glowed in the dark beyond the clearing.'

Noun String: This involves writing down one of each Noun type.

1. *creature* (Common)   2. *Kent* (Proper)
3. *colony* (Collective)   4. *Kim's torch* (Possessive)
5. *cottage* (Concrete)   6. *terror* (Abstract)

We now use this as a basis for writing the next stage in the story.

'*For a few moments there was silence, which was broken by a low buzzing sound. Suddenly a shaft of light beamed from the craft as a door slid open. In the shadows lurked a huge* **creature** *with long, grey tentacles. A chute descended from the door and the strange figure slid down it like a snake. Kim's eyes widened as it was followed by dozens more smaller creatures of a similar kind.*

So they had finally landed; visitors from outer space in the rolling hills of **Kent**, *the so-called 'Garden of England'. Just as Kim was contemplating the significance of this momentous event, all the aliens, except the first and largest, disappeared into nearby woods like a* **colony** *of ants.*

Kim knew she had to warn people. She eased herself back from the bush and switched on her torch to see her watch. It was 1.00am. The sudden flash from **Kim's torch** *was detected by the alien. Its enormous head swung in her direction and it shuffled towards her.*

Kim made off as fast as she could go. She could reach her aunt's **cottage** *on the hill in no time if she took the short cut along a steep path. Kim scrambled up the overgrown track and dashed towards the comforting lights of the distant house. Suddenly she tripped over some creepers, falling headlong and cracking her head against a rock. Kim lay dazed, until she felt a cold, slimy tentacle brush against her face. She opened her eyes in* **terror**.'

Exercise 7: 4

Create a Noun String and use it to write an extension to the **'Stranded'** story.

'*I drag myself up onto the sand exhausted. The sea heaves as the storm rages in the darkness. After choking and belching I finally cough up the sea-water from my lungs. For a moment I lie still;*

grateful to be alive. Eventually I lift my soaked and weary head and look out across the lagoon. The boat is breaking up on the rocks. It splinters, crashes against them again and then disappears beneath the waves. I turn and face the seashore. I peer into the darkness and can just make out the dim outline of palm trees...'

Noun String:

1. .... 2. .... 3. ....
4. .... 5. .... 6. ....

Continue the story:

....

....

....

....

....

....

....

....

e. Using a Variety of Nouns

Using varied and unusual Nouns can make your writing more interesting and avoids repetition. A thesaurus is a useful tool.

Example: Use varied and unusual Nouns to make the opening of the *'Aliens'* story more interesting.

*'Kim fell back terrified as the bright lights grew closer. The **forest** lit up and the **hum** became a deafening **wail**. She crouched down*

*behind the **bushes** and shielded her eyes. Suddenly the blinding **light** faded and there was **silence**. A large, disc-like **shape** glowed in the **dark** beyond the **clearing**.'*

The highlighted Nouns can be replaced with alternatives.
1. ***forest*** becomes ***woodland***   2. ***hum*** becomes ***drone***
3. ***wail*** becomes ***squeal***   4. ***bushes*** becomes ***undergrowth***
5. ***light*** becomes ***radiance***   6. ***silence*** becomes ***stillness***
7. ***shape*** becomes ***silhouette***   8. ***dark*** becomes ***gloom***
9. ***clearing*** becomes ***dell***

Note: In the original passage *'lights'* and *'light'* are used. To give more variety *'light'* has been changed to *radiance*. We can now review the passage with the changes:

*'Kim fell back **petrified** as the bright lights grew closer. The **woodland** lit up and the **drone** became a deafening **squeal**. She crouched down behind the **undergrowth** and shielded her eyes. Suddenly the blinding **radiance** faded and there was **stillness**. A large, disc-like **silhouette** glowed in the **gloom** beyond the **dell**.'*

Exercise 7: 5

Replace the highlighted Nouns in the *'Stranded'* story with better alternatives.

*'I drag myself up onto the **sand** exhausted. The **sea** heaves as the **storm** rages in the darkness. After choking and belching I finally cough up the **sea-water** from my lungs. For a **moment** I lie still; grateful to be alive. Eventually I lift my soaked and weary head and look out across the lagoon. The **boat** is breaking up on the **rocks**. It splinters, crashes against them again and then disappears beneath the **waves**. I turn and face the shoreline. I peer into the **darkness** and can just make out the dim **outline** of palm trees...'*

Here is a list of Nouns from a thesaurus that can be used to improve the passage. Write the words in the correct spaces.

© 2008 Stephen Curran

| vessel | contour | ocean | shadows | instant |
| reef | tempest | surf | salt-water | beach |

'I drag myself up onto the .... exhausted. The .... heaves as the .... rages in the darkness. After choking and belching I finally cough up the .... from my lungs. For an .... I lie still; grateful to be alive. Eventually I lift my soaked and weary head and look out across the lagoon. The .... is breaking up on the .... It splinters, crashes against the rocks and then disappears beneath the .... I turn and face the shoreline. I peer into the .... and can just make out the dim .... of palm trees...'

2. Pronouns

A **Pronoun** is a word used to replace a Noun. The use of Pronouns avoids repetition and improves the flow of writing. The following Pronouns can be used:

I	we	he	she	you	they	it	these
me	us	him	her	your	them	its	those
mine	our	his	hers	yours	their		
my	ours				theirs		

Example: Replace some of the Nouns with Pronouns in this extract of *'The Christmas Lights'* story.

'Angie awoke and found **Angie** was lying on a bed of silk in a glorious bedchamber. A single candle burned at an open window. A cool breeze made **the candle** flicker and cast eerie shadows on the sumptuously plastered walls. Angie sat up quickly, but **Angie** felt giddy again. A cold compress dropped off **Angie's** forehead and then **Angie** felt a hand quickly replace **the compress** and ease **Angie** back down onto the bed. Angie looked up to find Timmy's gentle eyes staring at **Angie**. **Timmy's eyes** flashed with concern.'

Pronouns are now used to replace the highlighted Nouns.

'Angie awoke and found **she** was lying on a bed of silk in a glorious bedchamber. A single candle burned at an open window. A cool breeze made **it** flicker and cast eerie shadows on the sumptuously plastered walls. Angie sat up quickly, but **she** felt giddy again. A cold compress dropped off **her** forehead and then **she** felt a hand quickly replace **it** and ease **her** back down onto the bed. Angie looked up to find Timmy's soft, gentle eyes staring at **her**. **They** flashed with concern.'

Exercise 7: 6

Replace the highlighted Nouns in *'The Ghost train'* story with Pronouns.

'**Rory's** day at the fair was very unusual. The problems started when **Rory** boarded the ghost train with his cousin Rhonda. The entrance was weird and colourful and **Rory and Rhonda** were very excited. The train carrying **Rory and Rhonda** trundled into the tunnel. The first few moments of the ride were exciting, but **the ride** soon became a terrifying ordeal. The large head of a monster with a cavernous mouth surged towards **Rory and Rhonda**. **The monster** breathed fire and **Rory and Rhonda** ducked down and screamed.'

3. Adjectives

An **Adjective** describes a Noun. It usually precedes a Noun but can occupy another position in the sentence.
For example:
'The **battered old** trawler arrived at the **busy** port.'
'The coal mine was **dark** and **scary**.'
Using interesting and colourful Adjectives can improve description in a story, but it should not be overdone.

Example: Identify the Adjectives in this short extract from *'The Christmas Lights'* story.

'Angie looked up to find Timmy's **soft**, **gentle** eyes staring at her.
   "You must rest Angie, there isn't much time. You'll need all your **remaining** strength."
Timmy sniffed and Angie noticed his eyes were **tearful**.
   Angie murmured, "What's wrong Timmy?"
   "It's nothing," he blurted, then hesitated, "well, I thought we might be **best** friends and now, well you've got to..."
He choked up and, broken-hearted, slumped onto the floor.

Angie shook him but Timmy just cried and cried. At last he rallied, sat up and pressed something into Angie's **open** hand, then closed her **tiny** fingers over it. As he did so, Angie's strength finally gave out and she drifted off into a **deep**, **restful** sleep.'

Exercise 7: 7 Choose from these Adjectives to improve this extract from the *'Stranded'* story.

picturesque, topmost, coniferous, spiky, luscious, sprawling, fierce, lush, running, blooming, beautiful, blossoming, uneven, ferocious, sharp, jagged, juicy, flowing, gushing, feverish, wild, sweltering, overgrown, steep, highest, verdant, scenic, perspiring, sparse, ripe

'The .... island stretched out before me as I stood on the .... mountain. I needed food and water desperately. There were .... trees and .... plants in every direction but was anything edible? Which plants were poisonous? I walked down an .... track that must have been used by .... animals. If I could make a spear with a .... point I could try and kill one. It would be very difficult and how would I ever cook it?

I heard the sound of .... water. In the clearing up ahead there was a stream. I was so thirsty I thrust my .... head straight in the water and lapped it up until I nearly choked. I looked up. There were some .... berries on a bush. I picked them and stuffed them in my mouth.'

4. Conjunctions

A **Conjunction** or **Connective** is a word that joins sentences together.
For example:
'Jim did not go to school on Monday. He had a cold.'
'Jim did not go to school on Monday **because** he had a cold.'
Using Conjunctions or Connectives permits the creation of longer and more varied sentences.

Example: Use Conjunctions to link sentences in this short extract from *'The Christmas Lights'* story.

'Icy air cut across Angie's cheeks **as** she woke with a start. She was lying on the sleigh once more, covered in soft furs **while** it bumped along the hilly, frozen wastelands. She lifted her head a little **and** looked back. Angie saw a tiny figure in the distance waving excitedly. Her eyes welled up with tears **because** she knew *it was Timmy. She waved back quickly **otherwise** Timmy might think she had not said goodbye. In front was the huge, burly figure of Santa, furiously driving his reindeer forward and onward.*

*Angie realised she was still grasping what Timmy had pressed into her hand, **therefore** she opened her fingers. Blue light flashed and glinted in the moonlight. Angie knew it was the priceless diamond **because** she had seen it in the centre of the crown. She gripped it tightly, **although** the journey went on and on for hours. Angie now knew she was safe **since** the warm feeling she had when she first saw the Christmas lights seemed to invade her soul.'*

Exercise 7: 8

Choose from these Conjunctions to link the sentences in this extract from the **'Stranded'** story.

and	before	although	otherwise	therefore	whether
or	but	since	unless	yet	if	because	until

'I stirred from my slumber .... found myself shivering violently. Darkness still enveloped the island .... the warm glow of the rising would soon heat the island. I felt desperately hungry .... I had eaten the berries the day before. Something more substantial was required .... I would starve. I struggled up and made my way up the beach and into the forest .... I needed to quench my thirst at the stream.

As I strolled past the trees, I heard a sudden rustling behind me .... I stopped to listen. As I turned around there was nothing .... I sensed there was something following me. There it was again; the snap of a twig .... I was hearing things. I started to run .... I felt terrified. Then I realised it was the thud of many hoofs. I had to escape .... I might be trampled to death.'

5. Verbs

A **Verb** is a 'doing' word. It is often the most crucial part of a sentence. It describes an action, event or a state of being.

For example:

'Robbie, the terrier, **bit** the postman as he **delivered** the mail.'

'Miss Thomas **was** my teacher in year six.' ('was' is the past tense of the verb 'is'.)

'Lola kept diaries for many years, but they **were destroyed** in a fire.' ('were destroyed' is a compound verb - two verbs placed together.)

The use of well chosen Verbs will help interest the reader.

Example: Indicate the use of well chosen Verbs in an extract from **'The Christmas Lights'** story.

'The sleigh **drew** to a sudden halt. In a moment Angie **found** herself right by the side of it. Santa **faced** her directly. His deep blue eyes **widened** with concern. Angie **felt** a pang of guilt. She slowly **lifted** her hand and **opened** the palm. The cold blue light of the diamond **twinkled** and its rays **floated** like sparkling waves of blue surf across his wrinkled features. Santa's lips **broke** into a broad smile; then he **chuckled** and **laughed** raucously. His guffaws **echoed** across the frozen landscape. Angie's feet then **rose** off the ground. As she **pulled** away from Santa, his lips **mouthed** something. The sounds **were muffled** and Angie strained to hear.

Whispers **drifted** across the vast expanse as she **gained** in height, "You **have** your wish; you **have** your wish."

Soon, Angie only **saw** a tiny red dot on the landscape. Seconds later, Santa **disappeared** altogether. The warm feeling inside her **burned** stronger than ever and Angie **cried**. All the pain and *loneliness she **felt** from the past weeks and months **poured** out. Once **purged** by tears of sadness, Angie **wept** tears of joy. She **knew** Santa's promise **was** real, but how **would** it be **fulfilled**?'*

Exercise 7: 9

Choose Verbs from the list to fill spaces in this extract from ***'The Ghost train'*** story.

crouched	hurtled	ruined	slammed	planned	halted
laughed	heard	erupted	veered	trusted	squealed
rested	scrambled	slipped	played	stirred	fought

'The large head of a monster with a cavernous mouth .... towards Rory and Rhonda. Scorching breath .... from the open jaws of the monster. Rory and Rhonda .... down and .... with terror. Suddenly the train .... left and Rory .... across the carriage and .... into Rhonda. The roars of the monster could still be .... echoing down the tunnel as Rory and Rhonda .... back to their seats. All at once the train .... and there was complete silence.'

6. Adverbs

An **Adverb** modifies (describes) a Verb. It answers questions such as *'how?'*, *'when?'*, *'where?'* or *'how much?'* with regard to a Verb. They are often followed by the suffix *'ly'* or *'ily'*. Well chosen Adverbs can greatly improve Description.
Examples:
The words *'extreme'* and *'quick'* have been modified with *'ly'*.
'Billy was **extremely** late and walked **quickly** to school.'
The words *'jerk'* and *'wary'* have been modified with *'ily'*.
'The dazed boxer rose **jerkily** from the canvas and stumbled **warily** forward towards his triumphant opponent.'

Example: Indicate the use of Adverbs in an extract from *'The Christmas Lights'* story.

'Angie's eyes opened **slowly**. The daylight from her bedroom window made her squint **blearily**. Her father brushed away beads of sweat from her brow. Angie coughed **hoarsely** and tried to sit up. She felt **completely** exhausted.

"Just a chill Angie. You'll be up and about by tomorrow."

Angie mumbled **quietly**, "I've been on a long journey."

"Yes, you've been in bed for three days."

Angie's heart sank **despairingly**. Now she knew it was all a dream. Nothing was different. Tears **gradually** rolled down her cheeks. She began to sob **uncontrollably**...

"Come on Angie, it's not so bad. Anyway you have a visitor from school. Apparently he lives just down the road from here."

Her father **nimbly** moved aside and a small boy **gingerly** approached. Angie had **hardly** noticed him in class before and had only sat next to him a couple of times. They had never spoken.

Her father **gently** commented, "It's Tim and he's **kindly** brought you a very special present from the class."'

Exercise 7: 10

Choose Adverbs from the list to fill spaces in in this extract from the *'Stranded'* story.

dangerously   desperately   furiously   carefully   briskly
thirstily   suddenly   quickly   extremely   patiently   frantically
thoughtfully   hungrily   knowledgeably   freely   hurriedly

'The thunder of hoofs drew .... close. I scrambled .... up a nearby tree. I was just in time. Wave upon wave of wild hogs rushed .... past, but I was safe.
My mouth was parched. The stream was only a few yards away. Silence; and then the return of birdsong. I clambered down the

tree and strolled ……………… over to the brook. I drank ……………… from the clear waters. As I dipped my head into the cool, running stream I ……………… saw a movement. There were fish. They darted ……………… across the stream attempting to catch the current. I was ……………… hungry and a fish would make an excellent meal.

I waited ……………… , my hands poised just above the waters. Then I made the grab; missed! A few more moments. I must be patient. Again my hands plunged ……………… into the stream. Success! My hands dragged up a sizeable fish.'

7. Prepositions

A **Preposition** links Nouns, Pronouns and phrases to other words in a sentence. Prepositions can be seen as describing the position of something or the connection between things. Examples:
'The school-boy walked **under** a bridge and **past** the shops.'
'The cat jumped **over** a fence and crawled **through** the cat-flap.'

Example: Indicate the use of appropriate Prepositions in an extract from *'The Christmas Lights'* story.

'Angie was startled at the name and sat straight up. Tim was very shy and bashful. He moved very nervously **towards** Angie. He slowly lifted up a bag, put one hand **into** it and drew **out** a parcel and gave it to Angie. As Angie took it, a card fell **onto** the bed. Angie opened the envelope, unfolded the card and saw the names of all her class were written **across** the bottom. In big letters **along** the top it read, 'COME BACK SOON ANGIE, WE REALLY MISS YOU.'

Angie eagerly unwrapped the present. As she tore **off** the paper she *realised it was just a theatre prop; a papier maché crown. It was encrusted **with** fake jewels. As she disentangled it **from** the wrapping, the largest diamond-like jewel came away in her hand.'*

Exercise 7: 11

Choose Prepositions from the list to fill spaces in in this extract from **'Aliens'**.

*across   behind   amongst   through   off   up   into   above
between   under   inside   over   around   towards   by   before*

We rejoin Kim as she runs towards her aunt's house in a bid to warn people about the alien invasion; but then it all goes wrong.

'*Kim scrambled up the overgrown track and dashed towards the comforting lights of the distant house. Suddenly she tripped over some creepers, falling headlong and cracking her head against a rock. Kim lay dazed, until she felt a cold, slimy tentacle brush against her face. She opened her eyes in terror.*

Kim stared .... what seemed like deep holes in the huge head of the beast. There were blue pin pricks .... these cavities and Kim realised these were the eyes. She could see right .... its head. It was completely transparent. Suddenly, it shuffled .... her. Kim screamed and the alien shrank back. Then she heard the sound of helicopters up .... All at once there were explosions all .... her. The creature appeared to shudder and Kim saw that it was afraid. Kim dragged herself back .... the rock. Tanks trundled .... the hill. The creature now made a whining sound and tried to escape .... the clearing. Kim now wondered if this beast was really a threat. It rammed itself up .... a tree and awaited its fate. Kim heard a shell whistle from the cannon of the tank; a huge bang and the alien was vapourised. Kim felt strangely sad.'

8. Interjections

An **Interjection** is a word added to a sentence to convey a strong emotion like surprise or pain.
Examples:
Ouch! that punch really hurt. **Hey!** you shouldn't hit people.
Ah! I've won the raffle. **Dear me!** That's a great surprise.

Example: Indicate the use of Interjections in an extract from *'The Christmas Lights'* story.

'"**Oh no**, it's broken!" Angie sobbed.

Her father reassured, "**Hey!** don't worry, we'll fix it darling." Angie stared at the jewel for a few seconds. There was a note too from her teacher, attached to the crown. It read, 'Angie, you've been chosen to play the main role in our Christmas play, 'The Snow Princess'.' Angie smiled.

"**Well I never**. That's my girl... **Oh!** and Tim says when you're feeling better he wonders if you'd like to go out and play." Angie's eyes met with Tim's and he nodded enthusiastically. They both grinned.

Angie exclaimed, "**Oh!** My wish really did come true."'

Exercise 7: 12 Choose Prepositions from the list to fill in the spaces in this extract from *'Stranded'*.

| alas | dear | ah | umm | oh | er | well | huh |

'............ food at last. I gulped down every last morsel of fish. .... it was not enough to fill me. I still felt the pangs of hunger. .... if only there was more. .... I knew if I was to survive on this island I would need to do more. .... and I once thought it might be fun to be alone on a desert island.'

Your Own Story - Draft One

This is your chance to write your own story using one of the following scenarios as a starting point.

On the next page are two story scenarios. Choose either:

Story 7 - **'The Spooky Mansion'** or

Story 8 - **'The Old Tombstone'**

- Use the learning points in this chapter to help you write.
- Write Story 7 in this book. Once you have learnt the principles, you can write Story 8 on separate sheets of paper.

Grammatical Devices

Try and include ideas and techniques from this chapter.

1. Nouns - Use a greater variety of Nouns.
2. Pronouns - Use Pronouns effectively to avoid repetition.
3. Adjectives - Use interesting Adjectives to improve Description.
4. Conjunctions - Use Conjunctions to create varied sentences.
5. Verbs - Use well chosen Verbs to create interest for the reader.
6. Adverbs - Use interesting Adverbs to improve Description.
7. Prepositions - Use Prepositions to improve sentence flow.
8. Interjections - Use Interjections to provide emotional colour.

In writing **Ghost Stories** the event (ghost) from the past that affects the present for the Hero Character can be a real ghost. For example:

In the famous Victorian ghost story **'The Turn of the Screw' by Henry James**, a Governess (Hero Character) is hired to look after two children in a large, old mansion. The former valet of the house, Peter Quint (Opponent) had a strong, unhealthy influence over the children, but died suddenly in mysterious circumstances. He returns to haunt the children and possess their souls. The Governess is childless and feels incomplete as a woman (her Suppressed Inner Need). Naturally, her maternal instinct makes her act to protect the children from the evil Peter Quint.

The painful event (literal ghost) from the past that affects the present (Peter Quint) relates directly to the Suppressed Inner Need of the Hero Character.

First Draft - Story 7
'The Spooky Mansion'
Opening Scenario told in Present Tense using First Person Narration:

'The wind whistles through the trees as the light begins to fade. Then we see it; the old mansion through the trees. It was all Pat's idea to visit what we thought was an old deserted house; an idea we would live to regret. As we approach, we spy a broken window in the lower storey of the house. We ease ourselves through the opening and find we are in a large hallway with an ornate staircase. Large white sheets cover the furniture and huge cobwebs span across every gap. A dusty portrait of an old man hangs over the fireplace. There is an eerie silence and a chill runs down my spine. Pat goes over to the portrait and looks up at it with curiosity. It feels like the old man in the picture is staring at us.'

First Draft - Story 8
'The Old Tombstone'
Opening Scenario told in Past Tense using Third Person Narration:

'No flowers ever grew near the oldest tombstone in the church cemetery. It was covered in weeds and leaned precariously. ..Name.. bent down, brushed away the dirt and tried to make out the inscription, but some of it had worn away with age. It read, 'Here lies Eliz (blank); an untimely death (another blank)'. ..Name.. looked more closely. There were dates, '1st May 1872 to (then nothing)'. Just as ..Name.. turned to go, he/she noticed there was a faint inscription in front of the 'rest in peace'. ..Name.. strained hard to read it. 'I will never.' ..Name.. shuddered as a gust of wind swept through the cemetery and the iron gate creaked on its hinges.'

Continue with either **Story 7** or **Story 8**, then use the Planning page to write down some more ideas for your story.

Planning - 1st Draft
Story 7 - *'The Spooky Mansion'*

Now let's write a story.

....
....
....
....
....
....
....
....
....
....
....
....
....
....
....
....
....

If you have chosen **Story 7 - *'The Spooky Mansion'***, copy out the opening scenario on Story Page 1 - 1st Draft, then continue your story on the pages that follow.

Planning - 1st Draft
Story 8 - *'The Old Tombstone'*

It's time for your own story.

If you have chosen **Story 8 - *'The Old Tombstone'***, copy out the opening scenario on Story Page 1 - 1st Draft, then continue your story on the pages that follow.

Story Page 1 - 1st Draft
'The Spooky Mansion' or
'The Old Tombstone'

Story Page 2 - 1st Draft
'The Spooky Mansion' or 'The Old Tombstone'

Story Page 3 - 1st Draft
'The Spooky Mansion' or
'The Old Tombstone'

Story Page 4 - 1st Draft
'The Spooky Mansion' or 'The Old Tombstone'

Story Page 5 - 1st Draft
'The Spooky Mansion' or 'The Old Tombstone'

Story Page 6 - 1st Draft
'The Spooky Mansion' or 'The Old Tombstone'

| Scores Out of Ten | Spelling & Grammar → ☐ | Creativity → ☐ |

Chapter Eight
The Seven Structure Steps

Structuring your story is about what happens and when it happens in the story. Story Events have to be carefully arranged in the right order to make your story work properly. All stories have a basic three act structure:

Beginning • Middle • End

This basic three act structure can be broken down further into **Seven Structure Steps** which form the basis of every story in the classic form. They are as follows:

a. Beginning

1. Set Up   2. Emotional Hook   3. Provoking Incident

b. Middle

4. Tipping Point   5. Crushing Reversal

c. End

6. Big Climax   7. After Effects

a. The Beginning

There are three Structure Steps which occur at the **Beginning** part of the story:

Set Up • Emotional Hook • Provoking Incident

These three Structure Steps are used to introduce the:

Context • Hero Character • Opponent Character

Stories vary as to where all this information is placed but, by the end of the first act, it must all be in position.

The Beginning of any story must introduce the following:

Context • Hero Character • Opponent Character

The **Context** is the relevant information we need to know before the story can start. We must know **Where** and **When** the story happens and **Who** is involved.

The **Hero Character** must be introduced as soon as possible as we must know **Who this story is about**. The **Set Up** should focus on your Hero Character's life before the story begins. We should understand the Hero Character has a Suppressed Need which is revealed by the Event from the Past that Affects the Present. A Conscious Desire, which may also be an Avoidance Behaviour, should also be evident. Identification with the Hero Character can be achieved by putting them in jeopardy, undeserved misfortune or likeability.

The **Opponent Character** should also be introduced. They too must have a Suppressed Need and a Conscious Desire. We may learn about these later in the story.

1. Set Up

The Set Up must have basic information about the following:

Context • Hero Character

The Context means Where and When the story is happening. The Hero Character must be established at the centre from the very start, so the reader is in no doubt who it is.

A story can begin in many ways, so it is possible to see the Opponent Character in the Set Up. There may be more detail about the Hero Character in the form of Flashbacks and Backstory and other characters may appear too.
The Set Up normally takes up about one tenth of any story.
The Suppressed Need, the Conscious Desire and Identification with the Hero Character can all be part of the Set Up.

Example: Using *'The Crash'* story, demonstrate how to Set Up your story effectively.

'John drove the new squad car out of the Police Station gates. It would soon be the end of his first shift as Police Constable John Vickers after a night on duty. However, he just had time to do some patrol work before knocking off.

A feeling of immense pride overwhelmed him as he sped down the winding roads towards East Street, where he once lived. Someone might even recognise him, he thought. In training he had received the highest marks for driving at high speeds of any new cadet that year. The award had pride of place on his dresser. At that moment he felt invincible. The buttons on his new uniform gleamed and everything seemed bright and cheery. He felt important for the first time in his life. Now everyone would respect him. The long months of training were over and the moment he had dreamt of all his life was here. He was savouring every minute of it.'

Exercise 8: 1

Think about the *'The Spooky Mansion'* or *'The Old Tombstone'* story again. Revise your Set Up for this story.

....

....

....

....

....

....

....
....
....
....

2. Emotional Hook

The **Emotional Hook** is the first major event in the story. It is important to 'hook' the reader emotionally as early as possible. This Event either provides some new opportunity or creates a fairly serious problem for the Hero Character. The Emotional Hook does not produce an Outward Goal in the Hero Character at this point, but their world is severely disrupted.

Remember: Identification with the Hero Character can be created by putting them in jeopardy or danger, making them the victim of undeserved misfortune, or making them likeable.

Example: Using *'The Christmas Lights'* story, indicate where the Emotional Hook occurs.

The Emotional Hook occurs very early in this story. Angie has travelled all the way to Glasgow city centre for her first meeting with Father Christmas, only to be disappointed. As a poor and lonely child, Angie has suffered Undeserved Misfortune and that draws us into the story.

'Angie stood on the corner of the busy high street holding her father's hand. He always wore his kilt on special occasions, even if it was freezing cold. Glasgow winters were always harsh, but the chill seemed to pass right through Angie. 'Oh Little Town of Bethlehem' blared from a nearby speaker outside the largest toy store in town.

Angie shivered and glanced back through the glass doors where she could see the cashier at her counter. She bit back the tears. Angie was still thinking about how amused the cashier seemed to be when she told her that Father Christmas had gone home for tea and he couldn't see her today.

Shoppers with bright, expectant faces and laden with last minute shopping of every kind dashed by. Their jollity only served to make her sense of disappointment all the worse. Angie had looked forward to Christmas ever since her ninth birthday, a full six months ago. Now there was nothing to look forward to or daydream about. Angie would now have to live her life in the here and now. Months of bleakness and boredom stretched before her. To Angie, this had seemed the only bright star on a cloudy and dark horizon. Now she felt really miserable inside.

Angie stared up above her. The dazzling rainbow haze of lights glowed through the falling snow. Angie had never been to this part of Glasgow before. The poor district of the city she came from had no pretty Christmas lights.'

Exercise 8: 2

Write an Emotional Hook for **'The Spooky Mansion'** or **'The Old Tombstone'** story. This is the new problem or opportunity for the Hero.

3. Provoking Incident

The **Provoking Incident** is the second major Event or turning point in a story. This is where the story really starts. The Story Problem is introduced and the Hero Character will have to come up with a way of solving it. The Conscious Desire of the Hero Character will be replaced by the Outward Goal.

| Story Problem is Introduced | → | Outward Goal of Hero Character Established |

This Provoking Incident can occur in one of three ways:
- It is caused by the actions of the Opponent Character
- It is caused by the actions of the Hero Character
- Something dramatic happens to the Hero Character which has nothing to do with their own or another's actions

Resolving the Story Problem will always involve overcoming the Opponent Character.

| Story Problem is caused by, or is connected with, the Opponent Character | → | Outward Goal of the Opponent Character Established. The Hero Character and Opponent will now fight over the same Goal |

Example: Write a Provoking Incident for *'The Sad Clown'* story that gives the Hero Character an Outward Goal.

'Billy notices there are dark stains all over Coco's beautiful blue and white striped costume. Coco lifts a can of beer unsteadily to his lips. More of it spills over Coco's chest and Billy recoils at the stench of alcohol.

Coco slurs, "That's just it, they don't work and you're just one little kid. What do you know?"
Billy pulls away. Coco looks up suddenly and sees Billy's eyes fill up with tears.

"Sorry, I didn't mean that."
Billy turns and runs away crying uncontrollably. Coco looks up. A huge, burly woman stands over him.

"Have you seen a boy called Billy?"
Coco shakes his head, then gulps more beer. She lumbers away.

Billy trudges slowly back through the orphanage door. He sees a shadow slide up the wall in front of him. As he tries to creep up the stairs, Miss Dagon is just behind; her tall frame dwarfs him.

"You disappeared! No tea tonight; you go hungry!"
Billy turns defiantly and faces her. Her eyes are red with anger. All at once she rushes forward and lifts a huge hand. Billy freezes in terror. Billy stares up at Miss Dagon. His large, soulful eyes fill with tears.

Miss Dagon hesitates, "Go to your room!"

Billy peers out of the window at the Big Top in the distance. His face tightens with determination. He now knows what he must do; run away; go somewhere no one would ever find him. Nobody cared anyway. He had money in his wardrobe and a small suitcase. Tonight would be the safest time to go; she would not discover he was gone until morning...

A small, lonely figure in a scruffy duffle coat stands looking up at the open window. Billy's knees are grazed, but he has made it down the drain pipe. He thinks to himself, it's the only home I've ever known. Billy feels confused. Surely there is more than this? The moonlight casts peaceful rays across the fields. Billy swings round, stares at the Big Top, and thinks of Coco. There is something about Coco he likes; but isn't he just like all the others? Billy isn't sure. He dawdles for a few moments, then trudges off decisively towards the Big Top.'

Exercise 8: 3

Write a Provoking Incident for **'The Spooky Mansion'** or **'The Old Tombstone'** story that gives the Hero Character an Outward Goal.

....
....
....
....
....
....
....
....
....
....
....
....
....

Beginning of Story Summary

Example: Using *'The Crash'* story, demonstrate how the Set Up, Emotional Hook and Provoking Incident link together to form an effective Story Beginning.

Set Up

The Set Up clearly establishes the Context of the story and the Hero Character. We see the Conscious Desire of the Hero Character and his Suppressed Need is hinted at.

'John drove the new squad car out of the Police Station gates. It would be the end of his first shift as Police Constable John Vickers after a night on duty. The shift would soon be over but he just had time to do some patrol work. His more experienced partner, P.C. Eddy Moore, lounged back in the passenger seat and seemed to be lost in his thoughts.

A feeling of immense pride overwhelmed John as he sped down the winding roads towards East Street where he had once lived. Someone might even recognise him, he thought. In training he had received the highest marks for driving at high speeds of any new cadet that year. The award had pride of place on his dresser. At that moment he felt invincible. The buttons on his new uniform gleamed and everything seemed bright and cheery. He felt important for the first time in his life. Now everyone would respect him. The long months of training were over and the moment he had dreamt of all his life was here. He was savouring every minute of it.

He realised Eddy had said nothing since they set out; he was normally chatty. John felt slightly uneasy for a moment. Then he had an overwhelming sense that he must prove he was up to being a speed cop. He felt Eddy didn't really believe in him, particularly after last night. He shuddered for moment and Eddy cast him a knowing glance.

"Something wrong?"
"No!" John quipped unconvincingly.'

Emotional Hook

The Emotional Hook causes us to Identify with the Hero Character because he suffers unfair treatment from the Opponent Character. The Suppressed Need and Conscious Desire of the Opponent Character are revealed.

'But there was something wrong. Just one thing had marred his blissful and rewarding first shift - Lee Noakes. John had forced him off the road about midnight after a short pursuit. A regular joyrider, he knew the routine: 'Step out of the car, spread your arms on the bonnet'; frisking the body; then handcuffs and back to the station for questioning. John winced behind the wheel as he thought of those embarrassing moments in the interview room...

Lee lounges back on the chair, his feet on the desk.
    "Get those down!"
He snarls and reluctantly slides them off, upsetting a cup. The coffee spills all over the statement.
    "Damn, now we'll have to do it all over again."
He belly laughs as John tries to rescue the papers. Eddy was standing right by the door. He had let John handle the interview and it was already going badly wrong.
    "You only caught me because the car stalled. Call yourself a speed cop... huh!"
    "Okay!"
John raises his voice. He feels the anger rising up within him. Somehow this fifteen year old kid is getting to him. He finally picks up his pen to start the statement again.
    Noakes jibes, "You were scared weren't yer?"
John blushes and looks uncomfortable.

"I ask the questions."

"I'm under age. I'm walking right out that door, whatever you write on that paper, in two minutes; and you know what, next I think I might 'ave a BMW away or a Porsche. You'll never catch me!"

"You'll kill someone!"
John knew his words sounded hollow.

Noakes smirks, "So what!" He pauses, "I like speed; it's all I got. There's no fun round 'ere, so I gotta make it."
Out of the corner of his eye John notices Eddy shaking his head. John knows it is a disastrous first interview...

John hit the accelerator and speeded up a little. Something about Noakes really gnawed away at him.

"Hey, slow down. What is it with you? When you need to go fast you go slow and right now you go too fast."
John ignored the comment but eased off. He knew that, even though he had been trained to drive police pursuit vehicles, he was scared stiff every time he switched on those blue flashing lights. Was Noakes right? He told himself he would get used to it, but what if he didn't? As John turned onto a dual carriageway he was confronted with a horrific sight.'

Provoking Incident

The Provoking Incident causes the Hero Character and the Opponent Character to establish their Outward Goals. Through the Provoking Incident the Hero Character is confronted by the Event from the Past that affects the Present.

'John felt a knot in his stomach as he slowed. It was a scene of carnage. Surely no one could have survived. The blue bakery van, its contents spilled all over the tarmac, lay on its roof. The stench of diesel was overpowering.

The wheels of the overturned van were still spinning as John leapt from his squad car. The flashing blue lights reflected in the puddles of freshly fallen rainwater. The van door eased open slowly and a blood-soaked hand reached out. John gasped in horror. It was his first day. He had always wanted to be a police officer, but this was just too much. John approached, then suddenly froze in his tracks...

The crash! Memories blasted into his head. Another fateful day; hospitalised for three months; a child on his own. Poor John, they had all said. Mum and Dad trapped in that car; the terrible mangled wreckage - their funerals. The bleak days of mourning that followed...

He realised Eddy was yelling at him, "Come on!" John went back into his thoughts. His father had been a police officer and would have been so proud of him. He couldn't let his father down; not now! He hadn't thought about this for years. What was on earth was going on? He brushed the beads of sweat from his brow and hurried to the door with Eddy. He saw the slumped form of the driver trying to ease himself out from behind a crumpled steering wheel. He was mouthing some words. John carefully supported the man's head. It was sticky. Eddy tried to loosen his clothing. The grey hair was matted with blood. The driver's breathing became shallow. For a moment he reminded John of his father. Then the breathing stopped. Eddy started mouth to mouth resuscitation and thumped his chest furiously; the blood, the blood; blood everywhere! John knew he was about to vomit; his hands were shaking; his head throbbed; he seemed paralysed.

John felt confused, desperate, and lapsed into a daze. He had worked so hard; been the best police cadet on record. Now it was all slipping away. When it mattered he was no good: a coward.

Eddy was now screaming at him, "Get on the radio!"

Then suddenly John snapped out of his trance. He had noticed a small movement out the corner of his eye. His eyes focused; there was another car. He hadn't noticed it before. It was about fifty yards further down the road and rammed against the barrier. A shaky figure emerged from the vehicle and swayed unsteadily for a moment. John flicked on his radio and spoke slowly.

"RTA at the junction of King Street..." he broke off mid sentence.
The driver of the vehicle was now tugging at it to pull it away from the barrier. The man turned round; then John realised; it wasn't a man; it was a boy. Noakes! And the car was a Porsche! Noakes limped back to the driver's door and tried to prise it open. John felt an intense surge of anger rise up inside of him.

John could see the flashing lights in the distance. He rushed back to Eddy who was trying to stop the blood. Then the man gasped, his eyes rolled back and he lay still. John knew that it was useless. This was now manslaughter. The man was gone! Noakes had caused it.

John watched Noakes ease himself back into the vehicle. The engine growled and burst into life. It revved up and moved off. Eddy jumped up and stood full square in the middle of the road. He held up his arm for Noakes to stop, but John knew he would not. Eddy's huge frame was no match for a sports car. He was tossed over the bonnet like a rag doll.

© 2008 Stephen Curran

John watched the car roar away, just as the ambulance screeched to a halt. Suddenly, there were paramedics pushing past him. Eddy was moaning in agony but John knew he was in the best hands. For a moment John hesitated, then he knew what he had to do...'

Exercise 8: 4

Re-write the Set Up, Emotional Hook and Provoking Incident for **'The Spooky Mansion'** or **'The Old Tombstone'** story. Refine and edit your material.

b. The Middle

The **Middle** of any story must have two steps:

Tipping Point • **Crushing Reversal**

The **Tipping Point** is the Mid-point of any story. It is that moment when the Hero Character has travelled too far and gone through too many difficulties to turn back. They are now nearer to the Goal than returning to where they began. It is signalled by a significant Event. An obstacle caused by the Opponent Character must be overcome if they are to move on.

The **Crushing Reversal** is the point in the story when the Hero Character appears to have lost everything. **The pursuit of the Outward Goal seems to have failed and the Opponent Character appears to have won.** The more desperate this apparent failure seems, the more satisfying the solution will be when it finally comes. At the last moment some important information will save the day, or a new opportunity will present itself to the Hero Character. This will give the Hero Character new Impetus to have one more try, and he will fight on.

4. Tipping Point

The Tipping Point is that stage in the story which, once passed, will mean there is no going back. It can be a moment of great danger or threat for the Hero Character. It will always have some connection with the Opponent Character.

Example: Using *'The Inferno'* story, demonstrate the effective use of the Tipping Point.

'Jim struggled up. The heat was unbearable. He clambered through the burning doorway. Flames encircled the staircase.

The acrid smoke was choking him. He slipped the breathing apparatus over his nose and made for the stairs. Beams and debris were crashing around him. He was terrified but there was something inside that impelled him to go on.

Suddenly there was someone beside him. It was Norris. He nodded but there was a glint of hatred in his black eyes. His lined faced was rigid and expressionless. They both knew they had to make the ascent of the stairs in one move and there would be no turning back. It was all or nothing.'

Tipping Point

'The flames beckoned. They both dived forward through the fiery cauldron. They made it. Norris was on fire. Jim beat out the flames; Norris shoved him away. Jim knew he had only risked his life so as not to be outdone. How could Norris turn this into a competition? But he had. They both ascended the steps carefully. Jim felt his body was burning up. Every sinew, every muscle, was searing. It was like being cooked alive. The stairs wound round. Would they be intact? He didn't know.

Norris was close behind. They made it to the landing. The smoke cleared a little and Jim counted the doors. He had seen the child at the third window. It must be the third door. He glanced back; Norris seemed to slow. What was wrong? What was he up to now?"

Exercise 8: 5

Write a Tipping Point for **'The Spooky Mansion'** or **'The Old Tombstone'** story.

....

....

[blank lined answer box]

5. Crushing Reversal

The Crushing Reversal is a point in the story when it looks like the Opponent character will win. The bigger the apparent defeat at this point, the more dramatic the winning of the Goal will seem after the Climax. The Hero Character will find a way out, but it is usually very difficult and dangerous.

Example: Using the *'My Dog Jack'* story, demonstrate the effective use of the Crushing Reversal.

This scene is part of the Progressive Conflict and it also becomes a Crushing Reversal in the Story Structure.

'The shed was no place for a long-term hideout. It was drab and dirty but, amongst all the rubbish, I managed to make a small space

to lay out the sleeping bag. Jack was restless and kept jumping up at the broken window. He wanted to run free but I knew they would all be looking for us by now. Jack seemed hungry all the time and I only had a couple of cans of dog food and a few biscuits left. It was growing dark and I finally had time to think as I lay on the hard wooden boards. All I could think to do was leave Jack in the shed in the morning and go and talk to whoever would listen; perhaps the police or the RSPCA? They mustn't find Jack until I knew he would be safe. Jack nuzzled up to my face and wriggled a little with pleasure. He felt safe but how long would it stay this way?

I was just dropping off when the darkness was pierced by some flashes of light across the ceiling. I could hear distant voices. Jack was at the door before me. I knew we were in terrible danger. We slipped out of the cabin and into the night. The tangled undergrowth felt heavy underfoot and it was so difficult to see. The voices seemed to be getting closer. We sped up, dodging between trees and bushes. Then I spotted them. The policemen were scouring the ground with their torches and right behind them were my stepmum and my dad. She must have guessed we'd come to the park; Jack always took his walk here. I just couldn't think of anywhere else. I ducked down as they swept past. Jack seemed to sense the danger and stayed close. One of the officers paused and pointed the torch in our direction.'

Crushing Reversal

'The beam suddenly caught Jack's eyes and he yelped.
    "Over here," one of them yelled.
I dashed into the bushes and Jack followed, but it was no use. A creeper lay across my path and I tripped, falling headlong. My

ankle twisted and the pain was unbearable. Jack licked my face in sympathy. Before we knew it, we were surrounded. The pain was overwhelming and then there were lights. The forest began to swim. I could hear my stepmum's rasping voice above the others.

"Stupid girl!" she snapped.
Meanwhile my dad was attending to my ankle.
The last thing I heard before passing out was, "Grab the dog and muzzle it."'

Exercise 8: 6

Write into **'The Spooky Mansion'** or **'The Old Tombstone'** story a Crushing Setback for the Hero Character.

Middle of Story Summary

Example: Using *'The Sad Clown'* story, demonstrate how the Tipping Point and Crushing Reversal link together to form an effective Middle to the Story.

Tipping Point

After this point the Hero Character cannot go back to where the story began. To succeed and achieve the Outward Goal becomes even more crucial.

'Billy approaches the circus trailers under a moonlit sky. He dodges between the stationary vehicles until he reads a small scribbled plaque on a dilapidated and shabby-looking caravan. It says, 'Coco the Clown lives here.' All is in darkness and Billy clambers in through the unlatched door unnoticed. He finds a corner and snuggles down under the costume rack. He looks up at the sparkling sequins on Coco's costume as the fading light catches them. He smells the greasepaint and he knows there is only one ambition he could ever have. He drifts into restful sleep and dreams of the future...

Billy is shaken roughly. He stirs and gasps in horror as he awakes to a face he does not recognise. Billy scrambles under the dressing table, knocking over makeup and face brushes.

"*It's me! It's Coco!*"

Billy peers out from under the table. He is shocked to see a balding, flabby figure with heavily-lined features. Billy recognises the soft blue eyes. They betray kindness. Coco shakes his head.

"*What are you doing here?*"

The trailer lurches. Billy realises they are moving, jumps on the window seat and looks out excitedly at the countryside.

"*Where are we going?*"

"*We are not going anywhere.*" *Coco retorts.*

Coco lifts Billy off the seat.
Billy struggles, "Put me down."
"Look, you can't come with us."
Coco lets Billy go and sits back bemused.
"I'm not going back. She's going to hit me!"
"Who?"
"Miss Dagon at the orphanage. I call her Dragon."
Coco remembers, "Oh yes, I've seen her."
Billy buries his head in his hands. Coco looks confused.
"You know, you're a bit like my son."
Billy looks up.
"His mother took him away years ago. He was about your age. She didn't want him to join the circus."
Billy pleads, "Then, you can teach me to be a clown."
Coco hesitates, smiles painfully and looks sad for a moment.

The trailer shudders to a stop. Coco pulls the curtain apart.
"It's the police."
Coco also spots Miss Dagon lumbering behind them with an angry pout on her face.
Billy tugs at Coco, "Please help me, don't send me back. She'll hurt me. Please?"
Coco considers for a moment then points to the curtain rail; Billy ducks down.

There is a sudden knock at the door. Coco half opens it. Billy hears muffled voices and sees Coco shake his head; the door slams shut.
Billy appears, sporting a red nose and wearing Coco's silver cap.
Coco shakes his head, "What have I done?"
Billy flings his arms around Coco and hugs him tight.
Coco checks the window again; he wonders when they'll be back.'

Crushing Reversal

At this point in the story something will happen that will make it seem as if the Hero Character has lost. They will need to take drastic action to save themselves and the situation.

'Billy stands proudly by Coco's side outside the circus arena.

The ringmaster announces, "We proudly introduce our new baby clown. Son of Coco returns!"

The crowd applauds wildly and Coco appears, riding his bicycle. Billy chases after him and somersaults as Coco slows. Then he steals Coco's hat and dodges all of Coco's attempts to retrieve it. The laughter is infectious. Billy trips Coco and he prat-falls headlong into a large tub of green slime. When Coco doesn't appear Billy pulls his fists to his eyes and fakes crying. Coco suddenly rises, dripping slime, and the chase begins again.

One spectator sits motionless. Her large, bulbous eyes watch Billy intently. Whilst the audience claps jubilantly her hands remain clenched in her lap. As the applause gets louder her eyes narrow and she begins to ring her hands uncontrollably.

Billy dashes from the arena, while the applause continues. He watches Coco stride towards him beaming broadly. He is the best clown in the circus again and all the other clowns know it; and Billy is responsible. Billy is happy now and he cannot wait for tomorrow to learn more new tricks. Everything is different. Billy thinks of that first performance...

Coco adjusted Billy's blue and white striped costume. It was identical to Coco's and Billy sized himself up in the mirror; Coco Junior, just a smaller version. Billy puffed out his chest with pride but he felt really nervous. Coco adjusted Billy's hat and patted his head.

"Don't worry, they'll love you!"
Billy wasn't so sure. He'd practised so hard. Coco was so patient when he got things wrong. The days of strenuous training, the bruises, the sweat and the endless feeling of tiredness; but it was all worth it. He wanted to be the best clown in the world, just like Coco...

Coco sweeps him up in his arms. He takes Billy to the entrance.
"Come on, it's you they want."
As they swing round to return to the arena they stop in their tracks. Miss Dagon stands full square in their way. She points directly at Billy. A knowing sneer creeps across her huge face.
"Do you know the penalty for child abduction?"
Coco blurts, "This is my son."
Miss Dagon smirks and then breaks into laughter.
"Billy, it's time to come home. Don't play games or I'll call the police."
Billy clings tightly to Coco. Miss Dagon makes to take him.
Billy screams, "No!"
Coco nods sadly. Billy holds onto Coco's arm; Miss Dagon prises him away. Coco's face paint begins to run as tears stream down his cheeks. Coco takes a step backwards.
He looks longingly at Billy, "I'm just a silly old fool; a coward. I'm sorry Billy... sorry."

Coco backs away. Billy watches him go and tries to follow. He cannot move. He feels the large hands of Miss Dagon firmly clamp his shoulders. Billy struggles but it is no use.
"Do as you're told or your ridiculous clown friend will be doing time."
Miss Dagon leads Billy away.'

Exercise 8: 7

Re-write the Tipping Point and Crushing Setback for **'The Spooky Mansion'** or **'The Old Tombstone'** story. Refine/edit your material.

c. The End

The **End** of any story must have two steps:

Big Climax • **After Effects**

The **Big Climax** is the high point of any story. **It is the moment when the Story Problem will be finally resolved. The Outward Goal of the Hero Character will also be met.** The Outward Goal is also adjusted to meet the increased Opposition. The Opponent Character's Outward Goal has also run its course. This usually results in the defeat of the Opponent Character - happy ending. A story can also result in the defeat of the Hero Character - tragic ending. Most stories end happily because we want to give the reader a positive emotional response. It is harder to do this with a tragic ending, but it can be done.

The **After Effects** of the story allow the reader to see the new situation for the Hero Character after the Climax. With no Aftermath, a story ending can seem abrupt. We need to give the reader the chance to get used to the new situation.

The Character Development can occur before or during the Climax of the story. It can also happen in the Aftermath, as a result of the Story Climax. As the Outward Goal of the Hero Character is fulfilled, their Inner Need is also met. The Self Worth of the Hero Character must be restored through what they have learnt. This will be a satisfying ending, even if tragic.

6. Big Climax

The Big Climax must be more powerful and Tense than the other four turning points, otherwise it will leave the reader feeling unsatisfied. It will seem like your story has a 'down' ending or ends in an anti-climax. Instead, the stakes must be higher, the Suspense more unbearable, and the desire of the Hero Character to win more desperate than ever before. Usually the action speeds up too, until the story is at fever pitch.

Example: Write an effective Big Climax for *'The Inferno'* story that will resolve the Outward Goal of the Hero Character.

At this point in the story, Jim the Hero character is about to experience a Crushing Setback. It will seem all is lost and he will die, along with the little girl, in the burning building. It will lead us to the Big Climax, the high point of the story.

A reminder of the Crushing Setback in this story:
'Jim had no time. The door was already ajar. He kicked it open. As he entered he could see the little girl slumped near the window. Her golden, fair hair was now charred and smouldering. Flames were creeping closer and closer to her tiny form. Jim could see she was still breathing in desperate heaves every few seconds. Falling to the floor had saved her, as the smoke had risen to the top of the room.

Suddenly, he heard the key turn in the lock. He couldn't believe it. Surely Norris didn't hate him that much?'

Big Climax

We move to the final stages of the story. It will now move to a Big Climax. This is the point at which the story is resolved. It will result in either a happy or a tragic ending.

'Jim made his way over to the prostrate body. He saw that she had tried to cover her mouth with a handkerchief but it now lay crumpled in her open hand. Jim beat out the flames around her and swept her up in his arms. He wrapped her body in a fire-retardant blanket. By now the whole room was ablaze and he was faced with a wall of leaping flames that reached the ceiling. Jim was now desperately afraid. Not just for himself but for this tiny child too. When it mattered he could never get it right, and he knew it.

For the first time in his life he prayed. If there was anybody there, he just wanted one more chance to do something with his life. If it ended now it would have all been for nothing. He thought about Julie, his little sister, lying on those rocks all those years ago. He just needed one more chance.

He cried out inside, "If you're there please help me God."

The blaze seemed to intensify. He could see the buttons on his uniform begin to melt. He held the little girl tightly and felt himself topple with the searing heat. He fell to his knees and lay as low as he could to bring the child under the smoke. The whole room was beginning to crumble. Flames shot up the walls like electric lightning; the floorboards began to curl; he could hardly see the window. This seemed their only chance of escape but smashing it would suck in the fresh oxygen. He knew they would be burned alive in seconds. There must be another way.

What about the door? He crawled back to it and hacked at it with his axe but realised in an instant it was a heavy-duty security door. Norris had known Jim would never get out alive. Thoughts flashed through his mind at a hundredth of a second. His last few moments on earth. There must be a way. Jim agonised and struggled to think. His whole body felt like it was burning up on the inside. His lips were so parched and his head so hot, every slight movement sent stab-like pains across his face.

"No! No, it can't be; I'm going to die," he mouthed.

Prayers are useless, it's all gone, he thought. The girl; he stumbled back to her. He would try to make sure she did not die alone; at least they could die together. He did not know if she sensed his presence - she was unconscious; but, although he deserved no solace, he would do his best to stay alive long enough to comfort her in death. Julie had died alone, falling in terror through the air until crashing onto those rocks. This child would not die alone. She would go peacefully to the other side of death's door, whatever that might be. He placed the breathing mask over her face for a few moments and felt her suck in air. Miraculously, she was still alive.

He knelt beside her; now everything seemed to move in slow motion, just like in a film. He thought, is this what it's like to die? The white haze turned blue and all the colours of the rainbow began to spout in all directions like multi-coloured Catherine wheels. For a brief second, all the pain and discomfort were gone and a sight of extraordinary beauty confronted him, as the flames leapt closer and closer. Then the terrifying fear returned - to be burned alive. He recoiled, lost his balance and reeled backwards. While on his back beside the girl, he looked up for the first time.

Then, he saw it. Through the haze and the smoke, a small trapdoor with a ringpull below it. He couldn't believe it; but it was too late. He was too weak. Jim thought he could never reach it but he knew he must try. There were only seconds left. There would be only one attempt. Jim would need to muster everything within him to do it.

With one gargantuan effort from deep within him, he jumped up, grabbed the girl, and hooked the trapdoor ring with his axe. It was stiff. He swung on it and he felt it budge. Then suddenly it gave way and an opening appeared. Loft steps tumbled through the flames to the floor. Jim scrambled up the steps with the child over his shoulder, dodging flames as he went. In an instant he was through the opening and he kicked the trapdoor shut. The smoke cleared and he realised the loft area was still intact. Smoke was beginning to waft through the rafters, but there would be a minute or two of safety. The loft window was small but they could get through it. Jim smashed the glass with his axe, fumbled for the latch and in a moment it was open. Seconds later the child was through onto a ledge. Jim pulled himself up and squeezed through after.

There they were... the firemen. They had not left him to die. The mechanical ladder swung into position and Barry held out a hand. Jim refused to take it until the child had been passed over. He caught Barry's concerned expression. He knew it betrayed some shame too for the way he had treated him. Jim refused his held out hand. Barry knew he could be enveloped in the flames. He signalled for the ladder to be withdrawn. As it swung away the roof of the building finally began to crumble.

For a brief second Jim didn't think he deserved to live. Then he remembered; he had saved the girl. He wanted to live! Jim jumped a clear three feet and his right hand clenched tightly to one of the rungs. His legs followed and he clung on desperately. The building imploded and disappeared in a massive ball of fire, but Jim was safe...

Minutes past; ambulances arrived. The little girl was safe. As she was taken away on a stretcher, Jim softly clenched her minute hand in reassurance. Her eyes flickered and then briefly opened. They were like deep blue crystals and glinted in the darkness. He felt her squeeze his hand and he knew she would live. For once he had done something right.

The paramedics tried to check him over but he pushed them away. As he turned to go, he noticed Barry and the other firemen standing

© 2008 Stephen Curran

around another stretcher. Jim approached and they stepped away. Jim knew it was Norris. Somehow they had followed him in and got him out of the building. There was no need for doctors. A white sheet covered the charred and blackened corpse but Jim could make out the facial outline and the huge frame.

Norris's gnarled, petrified hand gripped something. Barry prised it open and withdrew the key. They all suspected what it meant. They had found Norris slumped by the locked security door. Everybody knew how much he had it in for Jim. Some looked away; others hung their heads in shame.

Barry motioned to Jim, "We're sorry about everything." Jim smarted; then nodded knowingly. It was not the time for blame or recriminations. He did not want to be like Norris. He had back his self-respect and that is what mattered. The little girl was safe and he had proved to himself he could be a fireman.'

Exercise 8: 8 Write a Big Climax to **'The Spooky Mansion'** or **'The Old Tombstone'** story that will resolve the Outward Goal of the Hero Character.

7. After Effects

The After Effects will make the story feel complete. Sometimes it contains some explanation. We call this Exposition and it must be kept to a minimum. This can help round off a story and tie up any loose ends. It will show the new situation for the Hero Character and may indicate Character Development, if this has not already been signalled in the Climax.

Example: Write the After Effects of *'The Inferno'* story. This should close off the story and leave the reader with a positive emotional response.

'The applause was deafening as Jim ascended the steps in front of the new children's home. As he looked down at the crowds, he could see the little blond-haired girl at the front. She patted her hands together, sometimes missing, but her flashing blue eyes were firmly fixed on Jim. He knew her name now: Jessica - a beautiful name; it reminded him of Julie, his sister. Saving Jessica had given him hope for the future. Jim smiled as the silver trophy for 'extreme bravery in the call of duty' was handed over. He now knew that when the chips were down he had what it took to do it right. Jim now bristled with confidence. He had Jessica to thank for that.

Jim reflected as he stood in front of the applauding crowds; they were now giving him a standing ovation. The new building was complete. Now it was safe for the children to return after a full nine months. The money Norris had stolen from the project had been recovered from his bank account. Jim knew if this money had been spent on refurbishment of the building, as it should, the chances of there being a fire would have been more remote. The fire extinguishers would have worked and there would have been a new alarm system.

As he left the platform, the crisp, polished pips on his lapel shone under the midday sun. The firemen in Jim's unit made way for their new fire chief. Barry stood to attention as Jim passed by. Jim felt proud of his unit. More importantly he felt proud of himself for the first time in many years.'

Exercise 8: 9 Write the After Effects for **'The Spooky Mansion'** or **'The Old Tombstone'** story.

....
....
....
....
....
....
....
....
....
....
....
....
....

End of Story Summary

Example: Using *'The Sad Clown'* story, demonstrate how the Big Climax and the After Effects flow together to form a satisfying closure to the story.

Big Climax

'Billy dawdles at the orphanage door as Miss Dagon holds it open. The other children are all in bed and the building is in darkness. Miss Dagon's eyes narrow and Billy sees a fiery expression on her face. It is worse than usual.

"You're not escaping. Never, do you hear?"
Billy shrinks back.

"Now get to bed. Oh, by the way, as a punishment you'll spend all day tomorrow in your room and you'll only get one meal."

"I'm hungry now!"

"Too bad. Now go and take off that ridiculous costume."
Billy stands his ground. Her enormous frame towers over him.

"I'll never take it off. I'm going to be a clown and you can't stop me."

Before Billy can utter another word Miss Dagon pins him against the wall. Billy's silk costume is slippery and he slides from her grip and darts down the corridor. She gives chase, her large strides gaining on Billy's small steps. He makes for the stairs and the safety of his room at the end of the landing. Billy flings himself towards the door and tries the handle, but it's locked. Miss Dagon slows. Billy knows he is trapped.

They face off and she dangles the key in front of Billy's eyes.

"Now you're for it."

She lifts her right hand high above her head. Billy looks up terrified. It seems to hover in mid-air for a few seconds. Then it crashes down towards his face. The blow strikes him across the cheek. Billy is lifted *clear off his feet and catapulted against the hard wooden door frame. His head strikes the wood like a match. Then he feels himself double up; his legs lift off the floor; his whole body smashes down hard onto the floorboards. Billy feels warmth at the back of his head as blood trickles and oozes from his scalp. Then he drifts into a stupor and everything begins to blur. The pool of bright red blood forms a scarlet river as it flows away from Billy's head.*

Miss Dagon stands triumphant over Billy's tiny frame. A nasty grin spreads across her huge, bulbous face.

"That'll teach you to run away. Now get to bed."
Billy does not stir.
"Do as you're told, you little brat!"
Still nothing; Billy lies completely still.
"What have I done?"

"Indeed; what have you done?"
Miss Dagon swings round to find Coco facing her.
"What are you doing here?"
"You shouldn't be so careless with the door. It was ajar."
Miss Dagon ignores Coco; picks up the unconscious Billy, dumps him over her shoulder and rams the key in the lock. As an afterthought she bends down to wipe up the blood with a handkerchief.
"Just a minute," *Coco warns.* "That's enough! Billy's coming with me. And if you've really hurt him..."
Miss Dagon fiddles with the door. Coco steps closer.
"Go away or the police will know about what you did."
"And what about your brutality?"
Their eyes meet. Miss Dagon shakes with rage but she knows there is no way out; she is trapped. Coco pulls Billy away from her; at first she clings on hard, but then her grip gradually loosens. Coco cradles Billy in his arms and backs away.'

After Effects
Three months later

'The bright lights dazzle Billy as he makes his way through the hustle and bustle of preparations. Acrobats tumble across his path, jugglers toss balls and bottles into the air and trapeze artistes swing high across the arena. There is an atmosphere of great excitement. It is opening night and there is only one hour to go before the performance.

Billy is already in his costume busily practising his moves. He tries his somersault but tumbles badly onto the mat. Never mind, he thinks, he is a clown and it is supposed to go wrong. Then Billy remembers what Coco has told him. You can only do it badly when you know how to do it well. He picks himself up and runs towards the mat again, springs and bounces off the tips of his toes and flies through the air, then lands with a thud on his back. He spots Coco at the opening of the Big Top.

Billy gets up rubbing himself and slowly walks towards Coco; he knows it is the big day for something else too. Coco looks really concerned and Billy is now worried too. His pace quickens.
    "Are you alright? That was a hard tumble."
Billy nods. Coco stands motionless for a moment, then suddenly withdraws a letter from his pocket.
    "We've got it! You're adopted."
    "You mean I can stay?"
Coco nods. Billy runs into Coco's arms and hugs him. The circus band begins to play and performers start appearing.
    "Come on, son of Coco, we've got work to do."
    "Yes, Dad!"
They smile broadly at each other. Billy grips Coco's hand and they head off to put on their makeup.'

Exercise 8: 10

Re-write the Big Climax and the After Effects for **'The Spooky Mansion'** or **'The Old Tombstone'** story. Refine and edit your material.

Summary of Story Structure Steps

1. Set Up
This shows the life of the Hero Character up to this point. Where? When? Who? Hero Character Need and Desire. Potential Opponent Character is introduced at this point.

2. Emotional Hook (Turning Point One)
A problem occurs that upsets the world of the Hero Character and causes him or her to change plan. The Opponent Character may be indirectly involved with this situation.

3. Provoking Incident (Turning Point Two)
A Major Problem occurs that involves the Opponent Character. Outward Goal of Hero Character established.

4. Tipping Point (Turning Point Three)
The Hero Character cannot turn back after this point. The level of Conflict intensifies.

5. Crushing Reversal (Turning Point Four)
The Hero Character faces a major problem and it looks like the Opponent Character will triumph. At the last moment the Hero Character finds new strength to go on.

6. Big Climax (Turning Point Five)
The story moves to a big showdown between the Hero and the Opponent Character. After an epic struggle, the Hero Character normally wins the battle. Through the struggle the Inner Need of the Hero Character is met.

7. After Effects
The Hero Character is seen in their new situation.

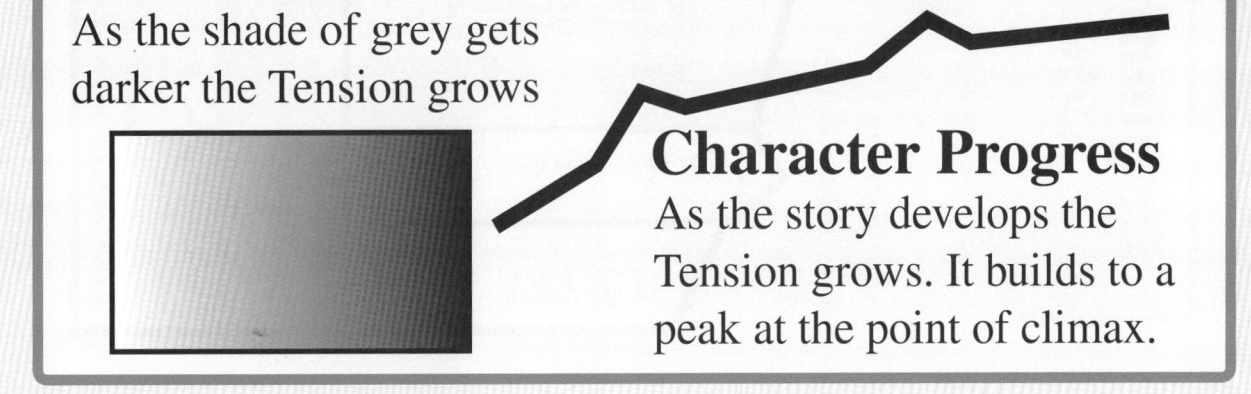

As the shade of grey gets darker the Tension grows

Character Progress
As the story develops the Tension grows. It builds to a peak at the point of climax.

© 2008 Stephen Curran

Story Structure Diagram

Beginning 25%

Turning Point 1

SET UP
- Context
- Where?
- When?
- Who?

EMOTIONAL HOOK
- Opponent Introduced
- Event from the past that affects the Present

HERO - Establish Suppressed Need; Conscious Desire; The Event from the Past that affects the Present; Avoidance Behaviours; Moral implications; Identification with the Hero Character
OPPONENT - Suppressed Need and Conscious Desire established

Turning Point 2

PROVOKING INCIDENT

- Outward Goal of Hero
- Suppressed Need
- Low self-worth
- Outward Goal of Opponent

Middle 50%

Progressive Conflict
Hero seems to make some progress
- Tension grows
- Some Suspense

It's too late for the Hero to turn back

Hero Character's Path to Self-worth

Mid-point Turning Point 3

TIPPING POINT

Progressive Conflict
Obstacles are more difficult to overcome
- High Tension
- Big Suspense
- Higher Stakes
- Obsessive Drive

Turning Point 4

CRUSHING SETBACK

Disaster strikes – the plan goes badly wrong

Opponent is winning

End 25%

New Impetus
The Hero makes one last all or nothing attempt to beat the Opponent and win the Goal

Hero adjusts Goal to still win out

BIG CLIMAX
Do or Die
Battle can be a real fight but any big Conflict can count

- Hero and Opponent face off
- Hero will usually win

Turning Point 5

AFTER EFFECTS
New Start for Hero

Hero Character regains Self-Worth

Life after the event shows how things have changed for the Hero

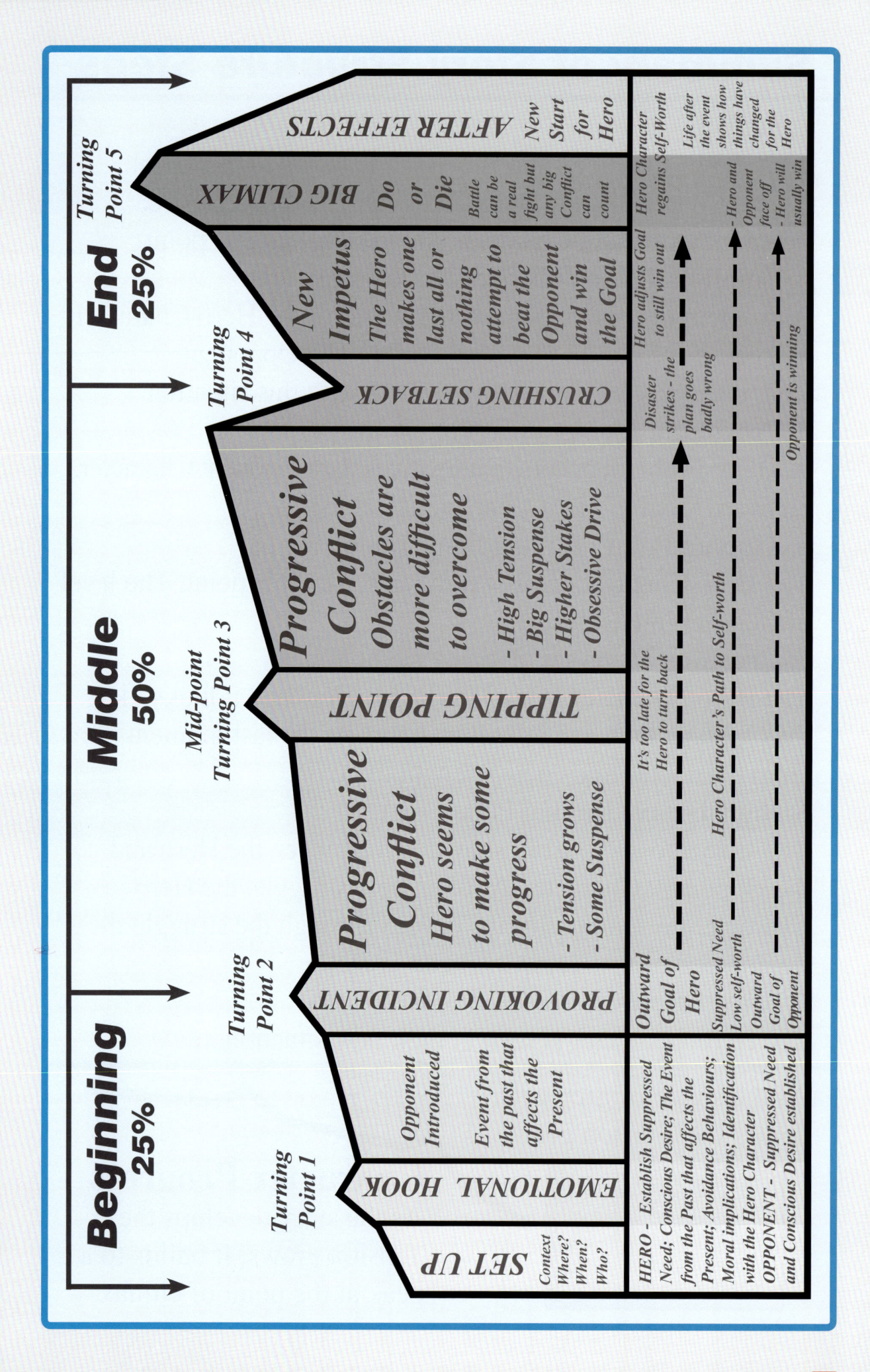

© 2008 Stephen Curran

Your Own Story - Draft Two

This is your chance to write your own story using one of the following scenarios as a starting point.

On the next page are two story scenarios. Choose either:

Story 7 - *'The Spooky Mansion'* or

Story 8 - *'The Old Tombstone'*

- Use the learning points in this chapter to help you write.
- Observe the basic rules below to help structure your story.
- Write Story 7 in this book. Once you have learnt the principles, you can write Story 8 on separate sheets of paper.

Structuring Your Story

Try and include ideas and techniques from this chapter.

1. Set Up - It is important to establish the Context of the story (where and when) and the Suppressed Need and Conscious Desire of the Hero Character.

2. Emotional Hook - This provides the Hero Character with a new opportunity or an initial problem to solve.

3. Provoking Incident - The Story Problem is introduced and the Hero Character will have to come up with a solution to it.

4. Tipping Point - This is the mid-point of the story. After this point there will be no going back.

5. Crushing Setback - At this point something will happen that will make it look like the Opponent will win.

6. Big Climax - This is the high point of the story when the Hero Character faces their greatest test. The Hero Character and Opponent Character will battle for supremacy.

7. After Effects - This rounds off the story and shows the new situation the Hero Character faces.

Observe these Rules and complete the Story

1. Use only three main Characters (Hero, Opponent and Ally).
2. Use no more than three Locations to tell your story.

© 2008 Stephen Curran

Second Draft - Story 7
'The Spooky Mansion'
Opening Scenario told in Past Tense using First Person Narration:

'The wind whistled through the trees as the light began to fade. Then we saw it; the old mansion through the trees. It had been Pat's idea to visit what we thought was an old deserted house; an idea we would live to regret. As we approached, we spied a broken window in the lower storey of the house. We eased ourselves through the opening and found we were in a large hallway with an ornate staircase. Large white sheets covered the furniture and huge cobwebs spanned across every gap. A dusty portrait of an old man hung over the fireplace. There was an eerie silence and a chill ran down my spine. Pat went over to the portrait and looked up at it with curiosity. It felt like the old man in the picture was staring at us.'

Second Draft - Story 8
'The Old Tombstone'
Opening Scenario told in Present Tense using Third Person Narration:

'No flowers ever grow near the oldest tombstone in the church cemetery. It is covered in weeds and leans precariously. ..Name.. bends down, brushes away the dirt and tries to make out the inscription, but some of it has worn away with age. It reads, 'Here lies Eliz (blank); an untimely death (another blank)'. ..Name.. looks more closely. There are dates, '1st May 1872 to (then nothing)'. Just as ..Name.. turns to go, he/she notices a faint inscription in front of the 'rest in peace'. ..Name.. strains hard to read it. 'I will never.' ..Name.. shudders as a gust of wind sweeps through the cemetery and the iron gate creaks on its hinges.'

Continue with either **Story 7** or **Story 8**, then use the Planning page to write down some more ideas for your story.

Planning - 2nd Draft
Story 7 - *'The Spooky Mansion'*

It's time to plan a second draft.

....

If you have chosen **Story 7 - *'The Spooky Mansion'***, copy out the opening scenario on Story Page 1 - 2nd Draft, then continue your story on the pages that follow.

Planning - 2nd Draft
Story 8 - *'The Old Tombstone'*

Let's plan a second draft.

If you have chosen **Story 8 - *'The Old Tombstone'***, copy out the opening scenario on Story Page 1 - 2nd Draft, then continue your story on the pages that follow.

Story Page 1 - 2nd Draft
'The Spooky Mansion' or 'The Old Tombstone'

Story Page 2 - 2nd Draft
'The Spooky Mansion' or 'The Old Tombstone'

Story Page 3 - 2nd Draft
'The Spooky Mansion' or 'The Old Tombstone'

Story Page 4 - 2nd Draft
'The Spooky Mansion' or 'The Old Tombstone'

Story Page 5 - 2nd Draft
'The Spooky Mansion' or
'The Old Tombstone'

Story Page 6 - 2nd Draft
'The Spooky Mansion' or *'The Old Tombstone'*

....
....
....
....
....
....
....
....
....
....
....
....
....
....
....
....
....
....

Scores Out of Ten | Spelling & Grammar → ☐ | Creativity → ☐

Marking the Stories

If you are working with a teacher, tutor or an experienced adult, the stories can be given a Creativity and a Spelling & Grammar mark.

Mark Scheme (marks 1 to 10)

Outstanding	**10 marks**	*Acceptable*	**5 marks**
Excellent	**9 marks**	*Needs some work*	**4 marks**
Very Good	**8 marks**	*Needs a lot of work*	**3 marks**
Good	**7 marks**	*Requires more effort*	**2 marks**
Satisfactory	**6 marks**	*Rework it completely*	**1 mark**

A mark below **5** means the story should be attempted again.

	Spelling & Grammar	Creativity
*Story 7 - **'The Spooky Mansion'** First Draft*	☐	☐
*Story 8 - **'The Old Tombstone'** First Draft*	☐	☐
*Story 7 - **'The Spooky Mansion'** Second Draft*	☐	☐
*Story 8 - **'The Old Tombstone'** Second Draft*	☐	☐

Total Score ☐ + Total Score ☐

Average Score out of 10 (Divide total by 8) ☐

Overall Percentage ☐ %

Total Score ☐

CERTIFICATE OF
ACHIEVEMENT

This certifies

_____

has successfully completed

11+ Creative Writing

WORKBOOK 4

Overall percentage score achieved [ ] %

Comment _____

_____

Signed _____
(teacher/parent/guardian)

Date _____